Midnight Flights

Audrey Jiang

BookLeaf
Publishing

India | USA | UK

Presentation by *BookLeaf Publishing*

Web: www.bookleafpub.com

E-mail: info@bookleafpub.com

ISBN: 9789358367287

First edition 2024

To my grandmother, who I never once stopped loving

To my mother, whose love made the universe seem finite

Coldly Intimate

Moon's gaze cast light upon her and I so
generously, but I wish'd it be day.
Streetlamps awake, hoping you'd find your way
Back, while we wait'd with cascading snow.

"Tick tock," said the clock, your return forgotten.
Twinkle twinkle, stars shone with fading lights.
Twice the weight two hearts carried past bright
heights,
Tiny stamps in white imperfection.

Hostile warmth welcomes frostbitten faces,
Pain'd pleads pale against your deaf ears. Love one,
And her loyalties lie safe with your stillness.
Disappear'd, expelled from your good graces
Forsaken, exiled away for frigid fun,
Yet my heart loves with granted forgiveness.

Evergreen

Intransigent pine,

Inculcating youth beauty,

Burdens eons of age.

Shutter

I envied those with pastel Polaroid cameras,
Where a push was all it took
To capture a frame,
A photo,
A snap of time in frozen bliss.

The colorfully plastic film
Only hanging from their string
By a wooden clip decorated
With messy frost.
The inanimate smiles

Of happiness in the miserable cold
Of bygone days. There's a slight glare,
A bearable heat, reflected
Off the crystalline snow.
There.

Their smiles look warmer,
Don't they?
Plastered against the white
Chill of space, an unsettling
Quiet sweeping panel by panel.
But it's frame rate never increases
Nor does it decrease, unlike what's
High in the sky, ruling machines
As a god. But even gods
Are limited in memory.

Tangible from a captured frame,
A photo,
A snap of time in frozen bliss or
Your god's choosing of a recording
Burned into deathless time?

Lovely

What is my mortal love worth?
For when my words cling
onto the air, they suffocatingly drown
in the silent reception of reciprocation.

The sun chases the moon,
day and night, night and day,
tirelessly across the vast
sky of clouds and stars.
It beams bright, illuminating day so
it becomes outshined by
beauties in the moon's dark
reign. It screams its affection,
Lending its raging light across
worlds, only so the moon will
Shimmer in all its glory.

Until it becomes smothering,
a temporary eschatological
conclusion as the sun finally
Seizes the moon;
eclipses of fire and ash.

The generations of birds raised
in the roof of our patio's corner,
nest elaborately woven with straw,
and mud, something so naturally
clear and complex. Seeing chicks and parents
Squabbling and cooing, sheltered every spring,
reliant on the roof's resistance against
hail and rain. The roof provides
without request, stability.

Until the bashing wind
Knocks the birds' coop out of
their nook, tumbling it across
the concrete in a clumsy dance.
The mourning doves refuse to
Return, with no fault of the roof.

Perhaps it be best
for it to be barely grasped,
before death.

Contrast

Falling snow fleets on soil,

Repeated shiver despite the coat's warmth.

Internal burning sparked in oil,

Petal by petal diffusing fever.

Forever

Crystalline flower

    Blooming before spring showers;

Innocuous details.

Pastime

Was it the ants scattering so
hopefully away from their mound,
Yonder over the settling mist?

And petrichor staining our lungs,
Removed of poisoned purities,
Enthralling a thousand gazes of

yearning for a violent peacetime.
Our obdurate presence–
Ubiquitous behind blurred panels.

Here lie the fallen petals of a previous
exodus, unable to escape the
Ravaging tears of God,
Eclipsed by us.

Potted Plant

Why won't my plant grow?

       Sky's rain and sun bless its leaves. . .

Oh! The pot's too small.

Apple Slices

Apples on a pure porcelain plate
Taste sweeter and crisper
Coming from your knife
Without fail.

Sister got stitches from
Pushing the blade far too hard
Into the apple core.
Slice, slice
So it slivers the apple and her hand.
All she wanted
Was that taste, while
She watches the apple-skin-colored blood
Drip, drip down.
Sister never liked
Green apples anyways.

I saw slices on my desk
Without fail,
Every night.
I see your smile
Without fail,
Almost every night.
I saw neither,
After our screams.
They stick in the air
And stare into my red core.
Yet, the silence afterward
is what stings
The most.

But the apples returned
On their pure porcelain plate
On my desk,
After the morning arose
Accompanied by an
Apology.

Disconnect

A fresh wind sweeps the dust,
And fear makes the clouds rain.
The sky doubts the land's trust.

It's nothing ever discussed:
The understanding of their divorced domain.
A fresh wind sweeps the dust.

Ravished by domestic wanderlust,
Sparks dissipated in vain.
The sky doubts the land's trust.

The nonchalant blue showers to rust
The foreign links of the couple's chain.
A fresh wind sweeps the dust.

The land's tears flow of sawdust.
There's no ignorance left to feign.
The sky doubts the land's trust.

Fissures fracture the desecrated crust.
Rain whispers the rumors to abstain.
A fresh wind sweeps the dust;
The sky doubts the land's trust.

Look

Raindrops   s p l i t   cloud'd skies;

Fish   d   under pond ripples;
     a
           r
      t

Lightning falls   a   f   a
r.

Daytime Kites

The grass grayed and slumped,
A wisened being shrinking with
Gravity's gradual tug.

Wind-carried laughter
Sweeping through the sunlit meadow
Warns the grass of what's to come.

A blade sighs its last
Bated breath and buckles beneath
A child's bastardly burden:

Flying a kite of
Kadeiloscopes, the tail string
Thicker than what a child could

Handle. The kite floats
And its iridescence brushes
Brighter against the white lilies,

Until it casts an
Inky dark over the child and
Meadow. The kite's tail rope wrapped

Around the child's wrist
Scathes the canvas skin, leaving
Trails of violets. It drags the

Child from Earth, closer
To the incandescent sun's rage,
Burning rose blush on pliable

cheeks. The child's head dips,
The irises blink. Nothing but
Clover remains in sight, and

Moonflowers stain lips
In silent decorum. Maybe,
the child will let go.

Fluid

Perching monarchs on

New drifting dandelion dreams,

Carefree as wind.

Blanketing the Wind

They'd be in bed by seven,
Falling asleep to her gentle touch and sweet hums,
Safe under their oriental blankets
Dreaming peacefully in her security.
A door closes and a lock clicks so quietly,
The sound drowns in the melancholic hurrying of the
wind.

Thunder's ephemeral drums brought by the incessant
wind,
Awakens the cherished child of seven
Years. It searches and tiptoes quietly
For any indication of her ethereal hums.
Conscious solitude shatters senses of security,
So it cannot be fixed, even under the warmth of the
oriental blankets.

The younger one's eyes see the designs of the oriental
blankets
Pulled overhead as wind
Beats against the curtained window, feigning security
In the children for seven
Minutes before boredom visits,
Dancing and humming quietly.

They'd whisper and breathe and mumble quietly
Under the safety of the oriental blankets.
They'd remember and replicate her sweet hums
Against the banshee-shrieking wind.

They'd pretend and play until the one younger than seven
Slowly slips into Slumber's transient security.

Again, the child remains alone without the confines
of security
And unlocks the door ever so quietly,
Stumbling in moonlight down seven
Flights of stairs without the oriental warmth of the
blankets.
Attempting to deafen the shrill wind,
The child hums and hums and hums

Until it is the one hearing hums
Of songs and dreams, rushing into the arms of
security.
Lightning's incendiary paintbrush brought by the
wind,
Shrinks inside and the world quietly
Seals and envelopes in the warm, oriental blankets.
The clock's hand leaps from seven.

The oriental blankets and her hums,
Quietly embed in gilt, fabricate security
As the meddling wind whispers warning seven.

Edible Arrangements

It started as a tiny black seed,
Sprouting from showered affection
To an oval of disparate Christmas colors—

stripes and tiles of muddled greens,
Bitter and shielding the saccharine nothing
Of nature's artificial will.

To criticize, it is a poorly made shield,
Used only for the ripening knowledge
Before its disposition discards itself.

The ruby crystalline interior is
Carved of the jeweler's responsibility.
Similarly uneven squares,

Triangles, and semi-ovals to be
Delivered with pronged chisels and
Metallic spoons ductile enough

For reform by curious hands of
Flesh. These unfamiliar shapes
All taste the same to me.

Necessity

Meadow of sunflowers

Harboring pollen fairies

Turn toward the moon.

Grown

I don't want a garden full of
Climbing tomatoes, pink raspberries,
Heavy blueberries leaping off
Their twig, or green onion sprouts
Poking out of the dark compost dirt.
I want a bonsai tree.

I don't want tall Chinese chives or
Lettuce and cabbage speckled with
Holes from the critters that lurk below
My roots or peculiar squash hanging
From the sky. I don't even want a
Field of small and deliciously
Plump strawberries scraping the soil.
I want bonsai trees.

So monstrously beautiful is
The sweet sapling plucked from
Nature's nursery by hands of unknown
Intent. A cracked branch with too
Many lines, a healthy leaf blowing
Against the wind, and bloodied
Capillaries litter the cement
Before the recovering sapling rests
In a hand-thrown ceramic dish with
White and grey smoothed pebbles

Gathering again. Contained and growing
Under watchful eyes that cut and
Contort the sapling when it becomes
Too unruly, taming the branches with
Thick scissors and twine. Cultivating
The cycle until the bonsai
Boasts an intrinsically
Perfect architecture.

That is a bonsai. Refined
Beyond taste and the humble garden's
Soiled abode, inanimate in a realm
Of aesthetics estranged from
Nature. Maybe, I don't want a bonsai
Then. Maybe, the garden will do.

Noodle Soup

There are the initial spices
that begins it all. The star anise floating
carelessly in the clearing, the gradiented
leeks rolling to the bottom of the boil, and
the Sichuan peppercorns of maw dancing
In the raging bubbling of the charred pot.

Meat, still marbled red and pink,
Tosses itself into heat, never to see
the kitchen light again as steam
Fogs the dew-dropped lid...

There's noise of an axe against wood,
machine-ly julienning the long carrots,
Dicing tomatoes, and cutting pastoral
leaves into perfect squares, despite thick,
indented middles.

The pot opens its mouth again,
Sighing tangible wisps of coiling air
in relief. The clean vegetable dives
Create splashes of broth. The last grey
strands curl out of existence with the
sound of narrow dough stripes

Slapping against the cutting board.
The broth simmers again, and the hand-
Pulled noodles slip in. The windows
are open on this warm summer
evening, and I see the lovely
aroma wafting away

I barely peek over the marbled counter,
the patience of a child tortured with deliciousness
Running thin.

Noodles in a
small, white porcelain bowl,
Hemmed in blue:
a final consummation.

Away It Goes

A well-oiled machine fit to perform
An unknowing simulation of
grinding gears and scratching wires tucked safe
in its programming against a storm

relies on nothing but the levers,
pushpins, and pixels its pilot wields.
Commandeered by instinct over fields
of strafing lights pivoting from stars,

the radio sputters to silence,
Favoring rocketing turbines
over a treading bridge; pooling in
vasts of kerosene, with layers thin

yet perilously unflushed. Erode
the underlying, bygone pseudocode,
But the dilapidated buttress
must confirm tomorrow's veneer of

Bluffing slats. "Fly airborne!" My pilot
orders, a bayard in the unbeknownst.
Fortunately, her jurisdiction
only extends far in my fiction.

To trust a consciousness fading in-
to senility with seasons past
Or the autonomous replies of
the pulleys' hushed rusting in tandem…

Post-Autumn

The first frost
glazes over my
Mother's tarp-
covered raised
beds. Autumn
graced gardens
of a time with
a yellowing
Summer.
The dimming of seasons smiled at the cherry
tomatoes
dropping from their lemonade vines; sun-kissed
Pumpkins; metal anchors uprooted from the
emptied soil by calloused, blue hands who
Planted them sunrises earlier. That's the
Last of them when there's nothing left
to bear. The nailed planks pose tall
Against the shivering winds while
The flippant vine-ropes curl to
nooses around the drying
bean pods' frames. Now,
My burden becomes
The graveyard. The
Vegetable graveyard.

Awake in Snow

A fiery warmth kisses the corners
of my mouth, a staining lipstick
Imprinted so long as the candle
of life pauses alight.

It burns my skin,
an embrace of flaming coals
Fanned by breaths, charring
the frosting air,

a refusal to be extinguished.
There's nothing of comparison,
for discarding warmth
in a blizzard makes for an

ignominious fool.
There's a pain
in every necessity,
even sacralized affection.